The Real Estate Safety Guide

The Real Estate Safety Guide

SURVIVING IN REAL ESTATE

James N. Roberts Jr

First Printing, 2015

ISBN: 1507772084
ISBN 13: 9781507772089

www.JimRobertsandAssociates.com

Contents

Introduction

I began my real-estate career in March 2005, after completing twenty-seven years as a law-enforcement professional in a metropolitan community with a population of three hundred thousand. I served as a patrol officer, a criminal investigator, an arson investigator, a homicide detective, and an administrative commander and retired as the chief of police of a five-hundred-member department. I am now enjoying a successful second career as a real-estate professional.

With that said, I am not trying to impress you but rather to impress upon you the years of experience I have dealing with the criminal element in our society. After beginning my new career, I soon learned that while real estate can be very rewarding, it can also be very dangerous. I quickly noticed my colleagues were extremely knowledgeable and up-to-date on the latest sales techniques; however, they gave little to no consideration to their personal safety while conducting everyday real-estate business tasks.

Because of my concern for real-estate safety, I began conducting safety seminars and personal safety coaching for local agents. I soon realized the problem was simply a lack of safety awareness about how things can quickly go wrong. Too many people involved in real estate are assaulted, robbed, killed, raped, and/or disabled each year because of criminal behavior. We all become very concerned when a colleague is murdered but later go back to business as usual thinking it will never happen to us!

The rate of violent attacks on those involved in real estate has continued to increase each year, and I do not want to see you or anyone else become a victim of a violent crime if I can help it.

Being safe while conducting real-estate business is why I wrote this book. It was no accident that I decided to title it *The Real-Estate Safety Guide: Surviving in Real Estate* and to use a red cover. Red is associated with danger, and simply seeing this red book on your desk each day should remind you to be prepared to survive. *think survival.*

The intent is to make this book a fast, easy read using bullet points in an effort to give you some safety ideas and to make you think. I know time is money, especially in real estate, and reading a book is not a top priority. However, your safety is important. Simply use what you think will work for you, develop a safety plan, and work your plan.

The safety suggestions I have made in this book are a compilation of my many hours of exhaustive research of thirty-six criminal cases from 1969 to 2014 against people in the real-estate industry across the United States. Many of the tips are commonsense; things we have all heard before but that have never been compiled in one publication. We must learn the hard lessons from others in the industry who have been victimized and incorporate those lessons into our own safety plan.

Anyone actively engaged in the real-estate industry should read this book. I know that some will think nothing has ever happened to them and that an attack is unlikely. But, while I hope nothing ever happens—other than a lot of sales—realistically, it is just a matter of time before that uneasy feeling presents itself. Therefore, I urge you to thumb through the book and attempt to pick up and review some safety tips and information. Who knows: maybe one idea will save your life! Or simply give a copy to someone who is just starting a real-estate career or a FSBO trying to sell his or her own property. They may thank you one day for helping them *survive in real estate.*

CHAPTER 1

Real-Estate Victims

Many real-estate professionals have been attacked, beaten, robbed, raped, and murdered while simply doing their jobs. However, I can assure you that there are many more attacks that are not reported because of fear of retaliation, humiliation, and public embarrassment. Unreported crimes against real-estate professionals and the public in general continue to increase each year simply because of fear and lack of confidence in the criminal justice system.

The *Realtor Safety Report 2011,* by Moby, S.A.F.E., and AGBeat, reported that 34 percent of real-estate respondents "occasionally" felt unsafe on the job, 2 percent "frequently" felt unsafe, 13 percent "never" felt unsafe, and 51 percent "rarely" felt unsafe on the job. The respondents felt most unsafe while: (1) viewing vacant properties; (2) during open houses; (3) working with REO, short sales, and foreclosures; (4) private showings; (5) meeting clients; and (6) coming out of office meetings. Based on my experiences in the industry and discussions of safety with other agents, I think the report is an accurate reflection of how real-estate agents feel about the issue.

In the United States, annual crime statistics are reported to the FBI for statistical analysis according to the type of crime committed, not the details relating to the victim. Therefore, it is almost impossible to identify crimes committed against real-estate professionals unless the crime is so brutal or unusual that it receives media attention. Minor crimes against real-estate professionals are seldom reported by the media, making it almost impossible to accurately track them.

Unfortunately, to learn from the experiences of real-estate agents who were crime victims, it is necessary to examine the crimes committed against them. The facts below represent the findings of the thirty-six cases mentioned in the introduction to determine how the rest of us may survive in real estate.

Case-Study Results

The most important lesson learned from this study is that, in all thirty-six cases, the attackers had a plan that was carefully followed to accomplish their crimes against their victims. The charts below identify important facts from the cases reviewed that may help save your life if you are faced with a similar circumstance one day.

Victim and Attacker Profile

Victim Profile	
Male Victims	3
Female Victims	33
Attacker Profile	
Male Attacker	36
Female Attacker	0
Prior Offenders	14

Female real-estate professionals were more likely to be attacked than their male colleagues; however, keep in mind that males can be victims, too. The attackers in these cases were all male, and almost half had prior criminal records.

Types of Attacks

Suspect Initiated a Planned Attack	35
Landlord Rent-Collection Attack	1
Spur-of-the-Moment Attack—Cell Call: Unknown Client	17
Spur-of-the-Moment Attack—Duty Call: Unknown Client	1
Met Unknown Client at Office	4
Set Up Showing with Unknown Client	3
Open House	2
Office Attack	1
Model-Home Attack	5
Attack During a Property Inspection	1
Known Client Attack	1

Once again, it is important to realize that criminals are not to be underestimated; they carefully plan their criminal attacks. *Almost half of the attacks were a direct result of the real-estate professional being contacted by cell phone for an immediate or spur-of-the-moment showing.* Attackers are bold enough to come to a sales office for an initial meeting with the real-estate professional and later attack during showings. Open houses and model-home offices are also easy targets for criminal attacks.

Types of Crimes

Murder	11
Rape/Sexual Assault	10
Robbery—Cash	15
Robbery—Jewelry	3
Robbery—Credit Cards	6
Felony Battery (with or without weapon)	12

Over half of the victims endured serious crimes against their persons, including murder and sexual assault. Many were also robbed of cash, jewelry, and credit cards. In addition, many were beaten, either with or without a weapon.

Types of Weapons

Fire	2
Hands—Strike Victim	12
Gun	13
Knife	7
Hands—Strangulation of Victim	6
Other—Sticks, Hammer, Fireplace Poker	4

The most common weapons used were guns and knives. The most unusual weapon in two cases was fire used to murder and destroy evidence.

Summary

Criminals have a tendency to specialize in certain crimes, and many learn new crimes and tactics from other inmates while incarcerated.

During my law-enforcement career, many criminals told me that they started out as minor offenders who committed property crimes and later graduated to drug crimes and serious crimes against persons, including robbery, rape, and murder. Most are drug users who must supply their habits, which can cost hundreds of dollars per day.

The criminal is always on the lookout for a way to generate money and locate easy victims who have the appearance of having money and valuables.

The most important goal of a criminal is to escape detection or arrest after committing a criminal act. A serial rape suspect once told me his only regret was leaving the victim alive after he raped her because she testified against him at his trial, where he was convicted and sent to prison for twelve years. Two of the real-estate professionals in the reviewed cases above were killed simply to eliminate them as potential witnesses.

CHAPTER 2

Victims and Criminals

Criminal Behavior

I believe a good defense makes for a great offense. It is necessary for you, as a real-estate professional, to have a basic understanding of how criminals think.

Do not underestimate the criminal. The advantage always goes to the criminal because he or she preys on the weak and unprepared, much like a shark in the ocean. The criminal will always have a detailed plan and will follow it to the letter to achieve his or her objective.

Crime is a learned behavior through associations with peer groups, family, friends, or other associates. Criminals learn their basic skills from each other. Jail is the greatest "crime college" I have ever seen. Inmates learn proven techniques from other criminals as they pass the time of day at the public's expense.

Hard-core criminals have long records and continue committing similar crimes. Contrary to popular belief, jails are not places to reform criminals or reduce recidivism rates. Criminals often exit prison more dangerous and hardened than when they entered.

Many criminals turn to crime to support drug-abuse problems. In the United States, our out-of-control drug-and-gang problem has been the driving force of "learned" criminal behavior today.

Criminals can act as a team. Criminals who work as a team can be extremely dangerous for real-estate professionals. Real-estate agents often work with couples (a man and a woman) when discussing or showing residential real estate and are therefore less likely to be suspicious of a couple. Sometimes the agent is initially contacted by a lone female who then arranges for an associate to show up at a listing or open house to commit a criminal act against the agent. Couples can more easily overpower a lone agent.

Criminals come in all shapes and sizes and can dress in whatever costume they think will not raise suspicions. The criminal who targets real-estate professionals has learned his trade from other criminals, associates, family members, and fellow gang members or from on-the-job experience. Don't let a uniform or other costume be a reason to let your guard down.

Things to Keep in Mind about Criminals

- Anyone can be a criminal; the criminal could be someone you know.
- Criminals can alter their appearance and identification.
- Criminals live and work in all neighborhoods.
- Crime is a learned behavior, usually from other criminals.
- Criminals are intelligent and will have a strategic plan to carry out their deeds.
- Most criminals have committed similar crimes in the past.
- Violent criminals usually have extensive criminal records.
- Criminals look for crimes of opportunity.
- Criminals have strong survival and escape instincts and will do anything, including murder, to ensure they are not caught.

Summary

It is not my intent to paint all criminals in a negative light. Some have been reformed and lead productive lives after being incarcerated. However, I have personally witnessed far too many who return to the life of crime they once knew. My description of prison being a "crime college" is accurate, regardless of the reform successes most institutions attempt to claim. For the most part, prisons and the criminal justice system are revolving doors cluttered with many of the same faces time and time again.

What I want you to remember is that the criminal has a definite action plan to carry out his or her criminal acts. He or she has honed this plan by learning techniques from friends and other inmates and by practicing on the street. The criminal will do anything it takes to avoid capture, including killing you. It is critical you do not underestimate a criminal who you think is about to attack you.

CHAPTER 3

The Real-Estate Business

All aspects of the business of real estate have different safety risks and potential dangers associated with dealing with people. It does not matter if you are male or female, weak or strong—everyone is vulnerable to attack. You must give thoughtful consideration to the role you play in the industry and any potential threats you may encounter. Start thinking about a safety plan and how you would react to a personal threat while doing your job.

It all boils down to working with and establishing relationships with people. Most people have only the best intentions and are interested only in conducting real-estate business. However, there are some who are looking for an easy target to victimize.

What services are usually expected by clients who are actively engaged in purchasing, leasing, or renting real estate, and what can we do to verify who we are working with from the first day? Verifying a client's identity is the first step of a good safety plan.

Meeting Clients

Real estate is 100 percent a people business. You must give thoughtful consideration about how you meet your clients.

Follow Your Broker's Rules for Verifying Clients

Does your employer or broker have a policy regarding how you are to conduct client meetings? If so, follow that policy to the letter.

Most initial contacts with potential clients are made by telephone. How you handle it from there is a critical safety decision. Do you require a face-to-face meeting at your office to get acquainted, or do you meet a stranger at a property? You may be tempted to meet in the field if you are convinced he or she is a hot prospect and will go elsewhere if you do not provide your services immediately. If not prohibited by policy, you should consider having a coworker, spouse, or other person accompany you when meeting a potential unknown client in the field.

Tips to Verify Clients

Insist upon prequalification with a lender. Most clients who are serious about purchasing a property can provide prequalification documentation from a lender or bank, which, in most cases, will provide positive identity.

Contact the lender to verify. Contact the lending institution to make sure the client's information is current and preapproved. Critical information can be obtained to verify what the client has told you.

Obtain renter and lessee information. However, renters and many commercial clients may not have documentation. A carefully drafted rental information sheet (approved by your attorney) and fund verification from a bank should do the trick. And verify the information provided by the client.

Ask, ask, and ask. Ask the potential client to fill out a client-information sheet. Do not be afraid to ask for prequalification documentation or proof of identity to ensure your safety. Start by verifying employment and residential status.

Check public records. Most states have public record searches available through the Internet and provide open access to a listing of sexual predators, as well as criminal records and civil records. Enter your client's name in these databases and search for results.

Check public tax records. Check the client's taxable properties through the Internet. If the client is listing a property, an identity should be available by simply checking tax records.

Check social networking. Many people have connections to social networks like Facebook, My Space, and so. Check out the client's profile information to confirm information he or she has given to you.

Obtain the client's driver's license number. Advise the client your broker requires positive identification for showings, and you need information for your insurance in case he or she rides in your vehicle during showings.

Make office introductions. Make sure you introduce your new client to someone in your office. Have someone snap a cell-phone photo of you and the new client if possible. If your office has surveillance cameras, the new client's photo will be captured automatically.

Note official clothing. Make note of clothing, name tags, and other items that could identify the client's profession. But remember, anyone can purchase or steal a uniform and badge and replicate a name tag and photo identification.

Obtain vehicle license numbers. As a new client leaves your office, walk the client to his or her vehicle and write down the license plate number and type, make and model, and color of the vehicle. Document the information on the client-information sheet as a precaution.

Follow company policy. Follow your company policy to the letter when dealing with clients.

If necessary, fire the client. It's OK to fire a client who does not check out or makes you feel uncomfortable.

Summary

Don't let your guard down when working with clients; be sure to verify, verify, verify, and verify again. The client may be attempting to build your trust so that you eventually let your guard down. Many times, criminals work in teams, so it matters little if you are initially working with a male or female or both at the same time. Stay focused and trust your gut feelings and perceptions about those who you choose to work with. Check them out first before working with them.

CHAPTER 4

Showing Properties

The most important duties of real-estate agents, property managers, leasing or rental agents, and owners who rent or sell properties is to show and list their inventory for sale or lease to the public. As we discussed in chapter 3, the key is to always know whom you are working with and to let someone you trust know what you are doing.

Once again, if you meet someone you do not know under that person's terms and conditions, things can go terribly wrong, as case studies have proven. Make sure you stick to your plan and meet new clients on your terms, not theirs. Remember, criminals carefully plan their attacks and will tell you any lie to accomplish their goal.

Not all properties are the same nor are all locations and neighborhoods the same. Careful consideration should be given before appointments are scheduled. Do not be lured to properties and locations you know little about; you want to stay in control of your safety.

Once you have verified your client or prospect, mentally review or modify your safety plan to fit the situation if you will be showing properties to them.

Pre-showing Tips

Be aware of your surroundings. Before showing a property, it is always a good idea to drive through an unfamiliar area to note any suspicious activity, vacant properties, and vagrants or other suspicious persons hanging around with no known purpose. Devise a fast escape route out of the area by both vehicle and on foot.

Discuss the property with the listing agent. Ask the listing agent about the property and discuss the layout of the building to formulate an escape plan if necessary. Do not depend on a listing sheet to determine if the property is still occupied and if utilities are on or off.

Use Google maps. This service will help locate and provide street photos of the property for you.

Know as much as you can about the neighborhood. Not all neighborhood residents welcome strangers. Residents can be very suspicious of unfamiliar vehicles and people entering the neighborhood. If the listing agent does not know about the area, do not be afraid to consult your local law enforcement agency.

Obtain crime trends in the area. Contact your law-enforcement officials to learn the crime statistics in the area you will be showing.

Understand types of properties. Real-estate professionals are required to show commercial properties, residential single or multiunit properties, all types of vacant properties, foreclosure properties, and raw municipal and rural land of all types. Each type of property presents different safety problems, which must be considered.

Establish a showing time. Establishing a showing time is a critical safety decision when working with an unknown client. The best course of action is not to show the property until you have had time to check the client and property out. If you do show the property, select a time when the greatest number of people are in the area; they could provide help if necessary. And *never* show properties at night.

Get descriptions of client's vehicle and clothing. When arranging to meet a client at a property, ask what color and type of vehicle he or she will be driving, what the client will be wearing, and whether the client will be alone. In a multifamily unit, try to meet the client in an occupied parking area to validate that his or her description is accurate.

Never drive an unknown client to a showing. Never allow an unknown client to ride in your vehicle to a showing under any circumstance. There is no difference between picking up an unknown client and picking up a hitchhiker on the side of the road. You do so at your own peril.

Do not show rural properties to an unknown client. Do not show rural properties to unknown clients no matter what their reasons may be to see the property immediately. I call these "now showings." Do not subject a colleague to the potential danger of riding with you as a safety net because it places both of you in danger. Do your due diligence and check out the client first.

Carry items of self-defense. We all carry items that can be used as self-defense weapons in an emergency. Think about what you carry on your person every day while doing your job, for example, keys, emergency-horn button on a key ring, pens, small knife, stick pins, flashlight, and so on. If you carry a weapon, make sure you have easy access to it if necessary. Understand and be aware that these items can be used as weapons against you too. Weapons will be discussed later. I strongly urge everyone to take an entry-level self-defense class to learn basic escape moves.

Showing the Property

Be in control when showing the property. Follow your safety plan.

Before Arrival

Dress in comfortable clothing that will not restrict your movements and wear shoes you can run in if necessary. Think about what you would wear if you were fighting for your life. Don't wear flashy jewelry and clothing or carry a large purse. Bring your cell phone, and carry it with you at all times. Don't forget to let someone know where you are going and what you are doing.

Upon Arrival

Park your vehicle for a fast exit if necessary. Don't pull into the driveway and allow the client to block you in from behind. Use your vehicle's emergency-horn button to alert neighbors if needed. Lock your vehicle to prevent someone from hiding inside while showing the property.

Arrive early and check the inside and outside of the property. Unlock all doors to allow for multiple escape routes if necessary. Check outside first to ensure the property has not been burglarized or damaged. Call law enforcement immediately if you suspect the property has been damaged or forcibly entered.

Arrival of the Client

When the client arrives, verify descriptions of the vehicle, clothing, and passengers if any. If multiple or unexpected people show up for the showing, if you cannot verify information given by the client, or if you feel uncomfortable, terminate the showing immediately and leave the area.

Only follow a client through the property at a distance, never allowing him or her to block your escape route. Never turn your back on a client during a showing. But do not assume you are safe by simply following the client through a home. It is still easy to attack a person who follows behind. Be on your guard at all times.

Never follow any client into a basement, attic, or upstairs bonus room because you are limited to one escape route. A criminal can easily trap you in these areas, and it can become your tomb.

Watch the client's *hands* at all times because the hands will be used to attack you. Also be aware that weapons can be concealed in heavy clothing, bags, or items carried by the client during showings.

If you feel uneasy about any client, allow the client to view the property alone at his or her own pace. Stay outside and away from the property and notify your office or an emergency contact person of the situation. It is safer outside rather than being trapped inside.

Other Tips

Robbery is a crime too many real-estate professionals experience. Consider using the bait-and-switch technique to outsmart a robber. Carry a dummy set of car keys and a money clip containing a large number of bills in your pocket. During the robbery, throw these items on the floor and make your escape.

Important: Keep an updated copy of all personal information you carry in your wallet in case you are ever kidnapped. Both sides of all cards should be copied and account numbers must be legible. Make sure your family or a trusted colleague can access this information for immediate release to the authorities for trace purposes if necessary.

Summary

Many of our case-study victims were found dead or injured at the same house they were showing. The interesting thing about these attacks is that most of the showings were spur-of-the-moment appointments in which a stranger called the real-estate professional for a now showing. I will readily admit I was one of the worst of-fenders when I first started my real-estate career. And many times I failed to let someone know where I was showing. I have since changed my ways, and I am now very cautious and suspicious of someone wanting to see a property *now*. I do not show unless I verify the new prospect first.

CHAPTER 5

Listing Properties

L isting opportunities come in all shapes, forms, and sizes. Many times, the real-estate professional will know the seller or lessor because of a previous business relationship. However, it may be helpful to recall if the business transaction was pleasant or difficult and plan accordingly.

There are times when referrals are made or a call is received from out of the clear blue sky by an unknown client wanting to list a property for sale or lease. Remember, listing property for sale or lease can be just as dangerous as any other real-estate transaction.

Listing appointments usually take place at the client's property. The property could be a home, a residential or commercial rental property, a vacant building, or a vacant urban or rural parcel. Each type of property has worst-case safety and security issues that you cannot control. The most significant problems for the real-estate agent are being on a stranger's turf and in a location the agent may not be familiar with.

I can see the scenario now: an agent receives a listing phone call. In the excitement of receiving the call, the agent blasts off to the listing appointment to meet the new client. Upon arrival, the agent enters the home to discover that the new client is a criminal who then attacks the agent.

Upon the first telephone contact with the new client, become a detective and ask many questions to help you verify the information given to you. Play the game on your turf, not on the client's. Please consider the following client listing tips.

Unknown-Client Listing Tips

Stay on your turf. If uncomfortable with your telephone interview, ask the unknown client to meet you at your office to go over necessary listing documents and property information.

Consider the listing location. Real estate is all about location, location, location. But so is your safety. Refer to "Pre-showing Tips" and "Showing the Property" in chapter 4 to help you develop a safety plan.

Use Google maps. Locate and obtain street photos of the listing using Google maps. This will allow you to verify the location and description of the property as given by the client.

Identify the client. Know your client. Refer to "Tips to Verify Clients" in chapter 3 to learn who your client is before you meet him or her. Use free Internet "people search" programs. There are many free Internet search programs to identify people throughout the world. Use these programs to establish the identity of clients who do not live in your area.

Check public tax records. One of the most useful tools all realtors have is online access to tax and property records that can easily verify information about property ownership. Use these records to obtain names and addresses of property owners and verify what you have been told.

Check public records. Most states now have free online data base listings for sexual predators by name and address as required by law. Log on to your local law-enforcement sexual-predator website to determine if the new client may be on the predator list.

Additionally, criminal and civil records are available, usually for a fee, from most clerks of court.

Listing Appointment Tips

Know the location. Drive by the listing location before the appointment to view the exterior and learn more about the neighborhood. Is the exterior of the home consistent with the caller's description?

Check that all the owners are present. Before setting the appointment, make sure all property owners will be present during the presentation. Do not be alone with the client inside a property. Reschedule if necessary.

Verify who the owners are. Make sure the client actually owns the property and this is not a setup to get you alone in a vacant property.

Check the status of the property. Ask the client if the property is vacant. If so, make sure utilities are on and functional.

Schedule the appointment wisely. The appointment time is critical. Most appointments are late in the afternoon to accommodate clients who work. If possible, do not schedule appointments at night unless you have another agent with you. Attempt to schedule on the client's day off when time is not an issue.

Give someone your location. Let your office and trusted people know your schedule and location. Don't be too proud to ask a colleague to accompany you on the listing presentation.

Summary

One agent in our case studies was lured to a property by the owner to write a contract, only to be sexually attacked when she arrived. She fought off the attacker with a pen and escaped as he followed her outside to her car.

Do not set up initial appointments with people you do not know at their residence or property. You can justify your request by having the client first come to your office to review listing paperwork and details before viewing their property. This buys you valuable time to verify personal information about the client and details regarding his or her property.

CHAPTER 6

Conducting Open Houses

If you open properties to the public, there is a definite need to advertise the open house to let potential buyers know the property is available for viewing on a specific day and time. However, advertising the open property could be like waving a red flag in front of a charging bull.

Criminals read the newspaper and surf the net too, and they see an open house as an opportunity to commit a felonious act on the unsuspecting real-estate agent. They may have seen a business photo of the agent on duty and may be attracted specifically to the agent holding the open house.

Remember, criminals are looking for easy, lucrative targets. If you place advertisements in the newspaper and on the Internet, making it widely known that you will be alone in an open house at a certain date and time, you make it easy for criminals. These advertisements are, essentially, invitations for them to come attack you. The word is out at the "criminal college" that real-estate professionals are easy targets who carry lots of money and credit cards, wear expensive jewelry, and drive fancy vehicles.

Recently my office experienced a potential dangerous situation with open houses. On several occasions the same two men driving the same vehicle attended open houses and acted very suspicious. They lounged on the den furniture, attempted to lure one realtor into the garage alone, and stayed for nearly the duration of the event.

Though the men made no attempt to attack the realtors, the intimidation factor and the interruption were real problems. It is not against the law to attend an open house; in fact, that is exactly what we want people to do. However, these individuals had no interest in purchasing a home. They only wished to intimidate or harass sales agents.

In a situation like this, the real-estate professional could obtain a peace bond on an individual who is disrupting the open house, directing him to stay away. An open-house waiver, drafted by an attorney, may also help. The waiver, signed by the property owner, would give the open-house realtor the legal authority to act on behalf of the owner of the property and advise suspicious people to leave the property or face trespassing charges.

However, if we know what is likely to attract a criminal, we can take steps to discourage a disruption or attack at the open property.

Open-House Considerations

Who wants the open house? Does your client want the open house or did you promise an open house as a listing condition? Often, for many reasons, clients do not want to have their properties open to the public. Some clients do not want the nosey neighbors viewing their property, and many are simply afraid of damage, theft, and potential burglaries. Discuss all the pros and cons with the seller first.

Conduct the open house with a partner. Consider conducting open properties with an assistant or another person, such as a wife, husband, or friend. If the property is in an area where you do not feel comfortable, consider hiring a security guard or off-duty law-enforcement officer to roam around the property.

Establish the ground rules with the seller. If the client does wish to conduct open viewings of the property, establish ground rules with him or her. You are the expert, and you need to make sure the client's best interests are considered and you are safe during the event.

Suggested Seller/Client Ground Rules

- Set the date and time period for the open house. Never conduct open houses after dark.
- Remind the client to plan on being out of the home during the open house.
- Store and lock up all medications, jewelry, guns, mail, or other valuable items because it may be impossible to follow each visitor throughout the home or property.
- Do not assume responsibility for theft during an open house or showing. Always have the property in showing condition, including the exterior, interior, and storage areas long before any scheduled showing by securing all valuables, medications, etc.
- Will there be areas excluded from public showings? Some areas may be excluded for safety reasons; if so, make sure those areas are secured.
- Discuss your safety plan with the client. Do not be afraid to let the client know that your safety comes first and that, if something does happen, it may become necessary for you to vacate the property until authorities arrive.
- Have the client notify the neighbors of the date and time period of the open house. If the client fails to notify the neighbors, it would be wise for you to make the notifications just in case something does happen.

- Have emergency backup numbers for your client in case something happens during the open house, and ask your client to have and monitor a cell phone during the showing.
- Ask the client to be sure that the driveway and the street in front of the home are clear of personal vehicles.

Open-House Tips

Wear appropriate attire. Dress appropriately by wearing comfortable clothing and shoes suitable for running if necessary. Remember: think about what clothing you would wear if you were fighting for your life.

Secure your valuables. Valuables such as jewelry, watches, rings, and purses should be safely locked in your vehicle or left at home.

Park wisely. Upon arrival, it is critical that you park your vehicle in such a manner to provide a safe temporary shelter or a fast escape if necessary. Vehicles parked in driveways can easily be blocked to prevent escape.

Meet the client. Meet the client at the property early to conduct a walkthrough to make sure the home is ready for showing and to go over last-minute details. Have the client return to the property at the end of the open house to allow you to turn the property back over and advise the seller of the response results.

Arrive early. If the property is vacant, arrive early to advise neighbors that you are conducting an open house and to be aware of any unexpected problems.

Carry safety devices. Don't forget your cell phone, video camera (if used), self-defense items, and your "bait and switch" kit (discussed in chapter 4).

Inspect the property. Immediately conduct your safety inspection. Before unlocking any doors, walk around the property to ensure all doors and windows are secure. Many vacant properties are subject to burglary, and you do not want to walk in on a burglar.

Plan escape routes. Before you enter the home, unlock all doors from the outside if possible. This gives you several escape routes if you encounter an intruder inside the home and need to make a fast exit.

Check utilities. Make sure the utilities are functional and all lights are in working order and turned on. Do not hold an open house without utilities.

Scan the property. Quickly scan each room of the property to make sure someone is not living or hiding in the building. Also make note of the floor plan and identify and unlock all escape routes.

Have a sign-in log. Have a sign-in log at the front door and insist that everyone who enters the property sign in. If you have a problem later, the sign-in log will provide law enforcement with a list of possible witnesses and the handwriting of the suspect. The suspect will never sign his or her real name, but the handwriting may be used by law enforcement for identification purposes.

Keep good notes. Make descriptive notes on everyone who enters the property, along with vehicle descriptions if possible.

Document visitors. Consider using a small video recorder to document all visitors who enter the property. Ensure you follow all state and federal laws regarding audio and video recordings.

Avoid traps. If you show visitors through a property, do not allow yourself to be trapped in a basement or attic space with no escape route.

Beware of groups. Beware of visitors who arrive as a group. Stepping outside to make a phone call may be the best response in this situation.

Beware of late visitors. At the end of the open house, if the client will not be returning, be careful of visitors arriving late or after the advertised closing time of the open property. It is possible you could be trapped alone. It would be best to refuse to show the property and to set up a personal showing later.

End the open house on time. Once the open house is over, ensure all visitors have left the property, quickly load all personal items in your vehicle, turn off all lights, exit the property, and lock doors from the outside. Do not reopen the property for anyone other than the owner.

Have an open-house waiver. Consider developing an open-house waiver form that gives you legal authority to ask someone to leave the property if he or she is acting suspicious. The form will allow law enforcement to make arrests if necessary.

Summary

The *Realtor Safety Report 2011*, mentioned in chapter 1, indicated real-estate agents felt most unsafe while (1) viewing vacant properties and (2) during open houses. Both situations exhibit almost the same characteristics of the unknown. You don't know who may be inside a vacant property upon your arrival, and you don't know who will attend an open house. Many agents have told me that they feel very unsafe in a vacant property they are holding open because they do not feel in control of the situation or the people who are attending.

I am extremely concerned with all aspects of open houses, model-home tours, or off-site office locations within a development because of safety considerations. Usually these locations are sparsely populated and are staffed with only one or two persons who are extremely vulnerable to attack.

If you must conduct open houses, think about the worst-case scenarios, use the safety tips, and devise your open-house safety plan.

CHAPTER 7

Dealing with Difficult Properties and Clients

As we have discussed, real-estate professionals deal with all types of properties and clients that may present safety issues. You cannot please all clients, and some may become hostile toward you as an agent. And there are those properties that present safety issues that cannot be ignored. The real-estate professional must be on constant alert, never letting his or her guard down and in tune with that little voice that says, "This may not be a good idea."

I wish I could assure you that if you follow every safety tip I have listed, you will always be 100 percent safe while conducting your real-estate business. Well, I can't do that. I do believe if you follow these tips, you will become a more difficult target. I can tell you from my twenty-five years of experience as a police officer that our way of life in America has drastically changed. I have seen firsthand the negative changes in my local neighborhoods. I have also talked to other law-enforcement professionals from all over the United States who confirm that the same events are taking place in their communities too.

Every day, real-estate professionals must deal with difficult real-estate clients, situations, and properties that test their abilities.

What follows are some of these problematic properties and the challenges they present for the real-estate professional.

Viewing Vacant Properties

Real-estate professionals, property managers, and leasing agents are often in the position of being alone at a property: viewing vacant properties for clients who are looking for a specific property, conducting inspections, taking photos, conducting security checks, or simply familiarizing themselves with listings in a particular area. These activities, which are major functions required of real-estate professionals, are some of the most dangerous duties performed by agents. According to the *Realtor Safety Report 2011*, these solitary activities were the most feared by the real-estate agents polled. However, there are things that can be done to enhance safety while performing these duties.

Vacant Property Safety Checklist

Obtain permission to enter. Before traveling to the property, contact the owner or listing agent to ensure the property is actually vacant and get approval to be on the property.

Inform others. Let someone know what you are doing, where you will be, and when you should complete the task. Always carry your cell phone in case you need emergency help.

Know the details. Make sure you know exactly why the property is vacant to ensure there will be no problems with prior tenants. Ask the owner about the neighborhood if you are not familiar with the area.

Ensure utilities are on. Ensure the utilities are turned on and the lights work properly. Never enter a structure without lights. Bring a good working flashlight in case of a power failure.

Dress for the occasion. Dress for the task at hand. Wear comfortable clothing and shoes suitable for running if necessary.

Carry self-defense weapons. If you normally carry a self-defense weapon, don't leave it in your car. Carry the weapon in a manner that ensures easy access to it if needed.

Preplan your inspection. Drive through the neighborhood and by the property to ensure there are no loiterers either near or on the property who may cause problems. Make mental notes of escape routes by vehicle or on foot if things go wrong.

Establish a parking plan. Park your vehicle on the street to prevent being blocked in so that you can quickly exit if necessary. Know the surrounding street names if you find you need emergency help.

In case of forced entry, call the police. Never enter a property without checking the outside for possible forced entry. Do not enter if you suspect someone has forced entry into the property. *Call the police.* Under stressful situations, it is natural for people to forget street names and house numbers. Write the address down and keep it in your pocket if you need to give it to emergency responders. *They can't help you if they can't find you.*

Enter the property with caution. Upon entry, always keep your back to your closest safe exit point and never confront anyone you may discover inside the property. Exit immediately if you see a trespasser and call the police. Many times, if the weather is cold, vagrants and trespassers use vacant properties for shelter.

Foreclosures, REO, and Short-Sale Properties

The collapse of lending institutions across the United States, a poor economy, and job loss have dramatically increased the number of foreclosure properties in most American cities. Many real-estate professionals have incorporated these properties into their businesses and have placed them on the market for other agents to show and sell.

Foreclosed properties can present many safety problems for unsuspecting real-estate professionals. Foreclosures do not just happen; someone went through the traumatic experience of having his or her home physically taken by a bank or lending institution. The home owner is usually distraught, angry, and obsessed with the situation when told to move out because the home will be sold to the highest bidder. Both the listing agent, who places a for-sale sign in the front yard with his or her name printed on it, and the selling agent showing the property are frequently identified as the villains by the former home owner because they are acting on behalf of the lending institution. This situation can become extremely dangerous if emotions overtake the situation and the real-estate professionals are caught in the middle.

Foreclosed Properties Safety Checklist

Follow listing/selling broker protocols. The listing broker or agent is responsible for ensuring the foreclosed property has been vacated by the former owner before the home is placed on the market. The property should be checked by the listing agent to ensure the previous home owner has been evicted or has voluntarily moved out. If the home owner has not moved out, leave the area and contact the lending institution to proceed with legal action. Never become involved in a confrontation with the former owner of a property.

Secure the property. Contact the listing agent to ensure the home is secure and all locks have been changed or rekeyed.

Discuss the situation beforehand. Discuss the situation with the listing broker to ensure that you will not be approached by an angry former home owner.

Protect the client. Inform your potential buyer/client of the details of the foreclosure. If the former home owner approaches *you* during a showing, leave the area and do not become involved in a confrontation. Inform the listing agent immediately.

Avoid contact with former home owners. If you have a scheduled showing and the former home owner is at the home moving his or her belongings, notify the listing agent and reschedule the showing. To eliminate the chances of a conflict, do not initiate contact with the former home owner.

Difficult Clients and Prospects

As a real-estate professional, you will sometimes deal with difficult people. The real-estate business can be a very emotional business, and dealing with people's property can be difficult because houses are usually the largest investment they will make during their lifetimes. Dealing with tenants regarding rent or lease payments, property conditions, and evictions can involve even more hostility. As hard as you may try, you simply will not make everyone happy all of the time.

Dealing with clients can become dangerous when tempers flare. When controversial real-estate issues arise, it is better to face them head on in an effort to arrive at a peaceful resolution among all parties.

Difficult Client Safety Checklist

Meet to discuss issues. Initiate a meeting with all parties involved, including all parties who have a vested interest in the issue at hand and your broker. Always keep your broker informed of the situation.

Meet at the office. Schedule the meeting in your office conference room. Never conduct the meeting at the client's location: it is too hard to end the meeting if things spiral out of control, and there may be access to weapons if meeting on the client's home turf.

Establish a formal agenda. Establish an agenda for the meeting and give each attendee a copy to ensure everyone knows why the meeting is being conducted.

Set the tone of the meeting. Set the conduct rules once the meeting starts. The moderator must immediately end the meeting if it gets out of control.

Stay on point. Stay on point; attempt to discuss and resolve the issues calmly. It takes two people to argue.

Secure the meeting. If threats of bodily harm have been made, it may be a good idea to ask an authority figure to stand by while the meeting is in progress and while all participants leave the premises.

Avoid an unplanned meeting. If a problem client appears at your office without notice to discuss a controversial issue, do not have the meeting on his or her terms. Schedule it for another mutually agreed-on day. This will allow you to prep for the meeting and encourage cooler, more rational behavior.

Tenants and Lessees

All landlords have difficult tenants who complain constantly about one thing or another; tenant complaints usually revolve around repair issues. Sooner or later, the landlord may find it necessary to evict a tenant who violates the terms of his or her rental or lease agreement. In some cases, the tenant responds the same way a home owner would who is facing a foreclosure. Even though the tenant is a renter and not an owner, the result is the same: the tenant loses his or her home or business location, which can be traumatic to the tenant and create a potentially dangerous situation for the landlord or property manager.

Some landlords insist upon collecting rental payments in person at the location of the rental property. Normally, if the landlord knows the tenant and they communicate well, all is peaceful. However, things can go wrong when problems exist with the tenant, such as late rental payments or violations of the lease agreement. One of my friends was killed by an angry tenant as he attempted to collect past due rent at one of his properties. The offender was tried, convicted, and imprisoned. My friend left a wife and young children.

If you are a landlord or personally collect rental payments from tenants, you must use extreme caution with problem tenants.

Landlord Safety Checklist
Know your tenant. Be cautious of tenants with desperate financial problems, late payments, multiple complaints, and so on.

Keep contact records. Keep accurate records on each tenant in case of an emergency.

Note suspicious behavior. Be aware of suspicious drug-related behavior when talking with a tenant. Learn what to look for if you suspect a drug lab is in operation on your property.

Never collect alone. If possible, never collect alone; bring a friend or coworker. Have the tenant meet you at a safe, neutral location. Let someone know where you are if collecting alone. Ask law enforcement to accompany you during difficult collections.

Carry a communication device. Always have your cell phone while collecting.

Carry a self-defense weapon. Consider carrying a legal self-defense weapon.

Evict problem tenants. Consider evicting problem tenants if there are legal grounds to do so. Do not become personally involved; file the necessary documents with the court and have law enforcement conduct the eviction.

Summary

Real estate is a business deeply rooted in relationships with people you know and many you don't know. Real estate is a fun and exciting career that can provide you with a great income if you work hard. However, you must develop a personal safety plan and listen to your sixth sense when something does not feel or sound right.

CHAPTER 8

Know Your Turf

Farm Areas

It is important to know the area where you will work most often. Most real-estate professionals will choose a "farm area" and will concentrate most of their time, effort, and marketing activities in that specific area. Farm areas can be a specific neighborhood, an active commercial or residential area, a new development, random investment properties, or historic real-estate areas.

Regardless of the area, you must have a good working knowledge of your city and know your local neighborhoods. If you are new to the area and do not know much about the city or area in which you are going to work, contact your local law-enforcement agency to obtain crime and neighborhood information before deciding on a farm area. Law-enforcement professionals work in these areas every day and can provide valuable information.

Many real-estate professionals are now listing and servicing repossessed and foreclosed properties in areas not familiar to them. Unfortunately, many of these properties are located in declining neighborhoods already suffering from high-crime rates and unemployment.

Many of these properties are being used as drug flophouses, meth-manufacturing sites, storage locations for stolen merchandise, or criminal hangouts. These properties can present dangerous safety problems for the unsuspecting real-estate professional.

Neighborhood Considerations

Rules and Norms
Each neighborhood has its own unwritten rules and norms that outsiders must learn and obey for safety reasons. Some neighborhoods will not tolerate door-to-door solicitations, vehicles parked in no-parking zones or blocking driveways, strangers approaching residents on their property, or strangers in unfamiliar vehicles driving through the neighborhood.

Crime Problems
Each neighborhood will also have crime problems, and residents' responses can be quite different. Many neighborhoods tolerate crime as a way of life, and residents will not get involved, act as witnesses, or lend assistance to someone in need for fear of retaliation from the criminals who live there.

Establish Yourself in the Neighborhood
One of the best ways to quickly learn about a neighborhood is to talk to the neighbors, the postman, the garbage man, delivery drivers, police officers, the newspaper carrier, and other realtors who have property listed for sale. Take the opportunity to meet these people to establish yourself and explain who you are and why they will be seeing you in the area.

Property Construction and Appearance

Know the basics of building construction to assess potential safety risks. Single-family homes are usually built on a concrete slab or on a pier-and-beam type of foundation with wooden floors.

Multifamily homes and commercial properties can be concrete and brick multistory or high-rise buildings. Many homes and commercial buildings have crawl spaces, basements under the main structure, and attic spaces that may or may not be accessible.

Structures can become unsafe to enter, and it is necessary for the real-estate professional to exercise extreme caution before entering or allowing clients to enter vacant structures.

Vacant Property

Vacant property can draw all types of illegal activity to the neighborhood, and these properties can and will be used by vagrants who stay there at night. Drug abusers may use these structures to have a place to consume their drugs and pass out. And curious children may also use these structures to play in. The real-estate professional must be aware that such things can and do happen in vacant properties and exercise extreme caution.

Gang Activity

Unfortunately, gang activity is present in most American cities. Many neighborhoods in the United States have gangs who may attempt to control their turf by force or intimidation. And due to the large numbers of home and building repossessions, many real-estate professionals are working in dangerous areas they are not familiar with.

Gang members set their turf boundary lines by using their identifying graffiti markings, and the members dress in similar attire. If gang members cross another gang's boundaries, a violent crime will more than likely take place. Many of these disputes result in drive-by shooting deaths, forcing the opposing gang to later retaliate to avenge the shooting or murder. The real-estate professional working in these areas must keep a keen eye out for gang signs and be aware of the potential dangers associated with gang activity.

In heavily controlled gang areas, it is important to understand there are *highly developed communication systems* in place to alert gang members to suspicious vehicles and people entering their controlled area. The goal is to inform members when rival gangs trespass on their turf or police come into the area to make arrests or conduct surveillance. Police often conduct clandestine gang and drug sweeps in high-crime and drug neighborhoods, which interrupt the criminal activity of the gang. Unfortunately, the unknown real-estate professional driving a strange vehicle may run the risk of being identified as a threat by gang members, thus resulting in a dangerous situation or bodily harm.

There have been cases where gang members have conducted surveillance on strangers who are seen in their areas. In fact, there are documented cases in which gang members have followed people out of their neighborhood to learn who they are, what they drive, and where they live and work.

Drug Labs and Production in Neighborhoods

Methamphetamine Labs
The methamphetamine (meth) phenomenon continues to grow throughout the United States. Meth is a highly addictive drug and results in extreme health and environmental problems. It is called crystal meth, ice, glass, or crank and is manufactured using over-the-counter cold medication, household chemicals, fuel, and a heat source.

According to the United States Drug Enforcement Agency (DEA), one pound of processed meth results in almost ten pounds of toxic chemical waste, which poses serious health and environmental hazards requiring expensive mandatory disposal. The invisible residue left from the production process will cause serious health issues, especially in children, if not properly removed.

Lab Locations

Illegal labs can be set up in houses, apartments, motels, hotels, private or commercial buildings, or any place that provides privacy. Meth labs have been found in all types of neighborhoods, and no area is exempt from being infected with a meth house.

During the cooking process, meth labs are *extremely flammable and can explode* at any time due to the chemicals used to produce the drug. Labs are normally quickly abandoned, leaving behind large amounts of trash, unused chemicals, and packaging. A building used as a meth lab is not safe to enter or inhabit until it has been professionally decontaminated.

Disclosure

The challenge for a real-estate professional is to recognize when a house or building has been used as a meth lab. Several states require meth houses to be decontaminated before anyone is allowed to inhabit the structure. Some states require owners to disclose that the home was a former meth house. Only a few states have set guidelines on how to decontaminate meth houses. The real-estate professional must know his or her state guidelines regarding meth-house regulations and disclosure requirements.

The following clues may help you identify potential meth-lab locations.

Keys to Recognizing a Meth Lab

Chemical stains on flooring or walls. Acids usually spill and splatter during the cooking process, leaving noticeable stains.

Burns marks. The cook may have burned cold medication packaging to eliminate potential evidence, leaving burn marks on the flooring.

Strong chemical smells. The smell of cat urine is associated with the meth-cooking process.

Noise at all hours. Neighbors may comment on a grinding noise coming from the residence at all hours; this is associated with the grinding of cold medication tablets to mix with the chemicals to produce meth.

Burned-out fire pits outside. Some cooks manufacture meth outside to reduce chemical smells in the house.

Trash and litter. Empty cat litter bags, plastic and glass bottles, and tubing strewn around are all clues. Cat litter is used to soak up chemical spills during the cooking process. Bottles and plastic tubing are used in the production process.

Coleman lantern fuel cans. Coleman fuel is used as an accelerant to supply heat to cook the drug.

Unusual building modifications. Look for exhaust vents poking out from odd places, like garages, windows, or outbuildings. The vents are used to release meth fumes and gases during the cooking process. Other modifications include alterations to sewer systems, which are commonly used to dump chemical wastes, and blacked-out or dark windows to prevent anyone from seeing inside the structure.

Cleanup

Meth-lab structures are serious issues for the real-estate professional. Simply cleaning the floors, painting the walls, and installing new carpet is not enough to rehab a meth house. It must be evaluated and totally decontaminated by a remediation professional before it can be safely inhabited. *Keep out* of a meth house; it's a hazardous waste site until it is decontaminated by a professional.

The DEA has estimated the cost of decontaminating a two-thousand-square-foot house or building to be in excess of $30,000. It is not uncommon for floors, sheetrock, ceilings, cabinets, and subfloors to be removed during the cleaning process. Some pier-and-beam houses, due to their construction methods, can become too contaminated to adequately clean and must be totally removed from the site.

Loitering

Many neighborhoods have groups of people who loiter on street corners, in yards, on sidewalks, and in front of homes, business-es, or buildings. These individuals, who may or may not live in the area, may intimidate those who live or visit in the area. They may be lawful residents or gang members establishing their turf or petty criminals who are visible during specific times of the day.

The real-estate professional must pay attention to his or her surroundings and not get into a situation of being approached by a group of unknown people. If you feel uncomfortable, the best course of action is to leave the area immediately.

Crack Houses

Sales and Distribution

Crack cocaine is one of the most destructive and popular drugs of choice in America and is usually distributed in neighborhoods from homes and on street corners. Many violent crimes are committed due to drug disputes between gangs, users, and suppliers.

We constantly hear media reports of drive-by shootings and home-invasion robberies associated with the drug trade.

People who occupy drug houses are often armed and can be dangerous if they think you are a fellow drug user trying to rob them of drugs or money or a law-enforcement officer attempting to conduct surveillance or take them into custody. The real-estate professional is not immune to being accidently caught up in such violent activities simply by being in the wrong place at the wrong time.

Crack-House Clues

- Multiple people visiting a home and only staying for a short period of time.
- Individuals exiting a home to deliver small packets to people on foot or in vehicles.
- Individuals who appear to be standing watch or guard in front of suspected structures at all times in all types of weather.
- Heavy foot and vehicle traffic in the neighborhood around a specific location.
- Individuals standing on the street who approach vehicles and hand small packets to occupants in exchange for money.
- Small plastic zip bags used to package crack for users.

Repossessed Properties

Within the past several years, real-estate professionals have endured an endless supply of repossessed or real-estate-owned (REO) properties due to the collapse of the mortgage/banking industry. Many real-estate professionals have built their businesses around the REO market and represent institutions that have foreclosed on clients who could not or would not pay their mortgages.

Due Diligence First

The repossessed property can be a very dangerous situation for the real-estate professional. The property should be vacant by the time an agent is selected, and it should be cleared to be placed on the market.

However, there are those cases where the property may still be occupied by a former home owner who refuses to vacate the house. The unsuspecting agent may be confronted by an angry former owner who identifies the agent as a member of the lending institution. This situation could result in a violent attack against the agent or representative.

It takes a significant period of time for the REO process to legally have the property vacated and cleared for sale through the courts. Some difficult properties may take several years to finally make it back on the market.

REO Dangers

During the REO time lapse, many things can happen to the property that can cause serious problems for the person selected to market and sell it. During my law-enforcement career, I have seen vacant properties used for the following purposes:

- Squatters who have nothing to do with ownership of the property may be living in it.
- The former owners may have moved back into the property after being evicted.
- A neighborhood gang may be using the property for criminal purposes or as a meeting place.

- Drug dealers and pushers may be occupying the property and using it as a crack house.
- It may be used as a meth house for the production of drugs.
- Vagrants may be using it as a safe place to sleep.
- Criminals may be storing stolen items in it.
- Drug users may be using it as a safe house to consume their drugs.
- The former mortgage holder may have vandalized the property or set it on fire.
- It may have been systematically stripped of copper pipe, wire, and aluminum siding.

REO Initial Inspection

The real-estate professional who handles these properties must be very aware and take extreme safety precautions when making his or her initial inspection. Here are a few safety precautions to follow during your initial inspection of a REO property:

Inspection Safety Tips

- Have another person with you during the initial inspection.
- Let someone know where you are going.
- Have reliable communication to summon help if needed and a good quality flashlight.
- Have a self-defense weapon with you (provided you have been trained and are proficient with the weapon).
- Be dressed for the occasion; wear comfortable shoes if you should need to run and expect to get dirty.
- If other people are around the property, do not confront them about trespassing.

- Never enter the property without first making a visual inspection of the outside of the property. Look for signs of forced entry (i.e., broken windows, open or unlocked doors).
- If the property has a pier-and-beam foundation, shine a light under the structure to ensure animals or a person are not underneath.
- Always knock on the door. If you hear movement inside, even though the property is supposed to be vacant, leave the area immediately. Do not confront anyone inside a REO property, regardless of the situation.
- Never inspect basements or attics alone.
- When you first see the property, always develop a fast escape plan based on how the property is designed.

The best tip is to call the police if you suspect anything out of the ordinary. Don't be afraid to ask for their help. Police officers will be happy to accompany you inside the property to ensure it is safe. Once the property is safe, have the REO representative secure it, if necessary.

Be smart when dealing with these properties. It is better to be safe than sorry; no REO listing is worth a confrontation with anyone who may be inside or on the property. Call the police immediately if there is a hint of a potential problem, and notify the REO representative of the situation.

Convicted Sex Offenders

Use legal public information. The criminal justice system now makes it mandatory for persons convicted of sex crimes to disclose their address and provide that information to the general public. State and local agencies provide this information to the public via websites specifically designed to conduct name and address searches.

The real-estate professional would be wise to use this search technique when dealing with strangers and potential clients and when checking farm areas. This technique is only for obtaining knowledge and to be aware of who you may be dealing with. Your clients should be made aware of these websites, just in case they wish to conduct a search, too.

Keep in mind that sex offenders may have legitimate needs for real-estate professionals, too. However, knowing someone is a sex offender may cause you to adjust your safety plan accordingly.

Know the Neighborhood

Neighborhood Crime Statistics

Major law-enforcement agencies in the United States capture and compile crime statistics for police use. Many of these statistics are available to the general public and may be posted on a public departmental website.

Real-estate professionals may use these statistics to learn more about crime trends in their farm area or areas they have been asked to list or show properties. This information will benefit the agent and his or her clients who may have little knowledge about crime in certain areas within their city.

Neighborhood Layout

The real-estate professional should know how to travel in and through the neighborhoods and areas he or she works.

Many times, circumstances take us out of our comfort zones into new areas we know nothing about. Maps are available online with all streets clearly marked. Pay close attention to entrances, exits, dead-end streets, cul-de-sacs, and traffic circles because, in case of an emergency, you could become trapped on certain streets.

It may benefit the agent working in an unfamiliar farm area to arrive early and drive around a bit while waiting on a client. That will allow the agent to get a feel for the area and develop an escape plan if necessary.

Summary

The point of this chapter is to remind you that no two neighborhoods or commercial areas are alike. All present unique safety challenges for anyone in the real-estate field. You must think outside the box and consider what could happen—because it is not a case of *if* it will happen but *when* it will happen. The key is to work as safely as possible, have a plan, and not be afraid to call the police for help if necessary. And remember meth houses are very dangerous to enter, expensive to clean up, and must be disclosed as meth houses.

CHAPTER 9

Safety at the Office

So you think your office is a safe haven? Not necessarily. Most real-estate offices have nice lobbies, and guests are greeted by a professional receptionist who may or may not be familiar with emergency office procedures—assuming the office has emergency procedures!

There are many occasions when an attack is planned and carried out specifically at an office. The real-estate office, broker's office, rental or leasing office, mortgage office, contractor's office, or title company office could be targeted by anyone who felt that he or she got a raw deal in a real-estate transaction. The media constantly reminds us of violent attacks in which deranged employees who have been fired or laid off commit murders. Usually, these attacks are directed toward the upper management of the organization, but there are times when everyone becomes a target.

This chapter helps you become aware of safety issues while you are in the office. Of course, if your office has rules and regulations regarding office use and safety, please follow your procedure manual.

After-Hours Office Use

Most real-estate offices have regular business hours. However, many agents work long hours after the normal business day ends and use the office to conduct business after hours. This is a dangerous practice and should be avoided if at all possible. If you must occupy the office after hours, here are a few safety tips.

After-Hours Office-Use Tips

- If you arrive at the office after hours, drive around the building or area to ensure no strange vehicles or people are hanging around for no legitimate reason.
- As you drive around the office, check for broken windows or open doors, which may indicate a burglary (possibly in progress).
- Are the night-lights on inside and outside the building?
- If you see a fellow agent's vehicle in the parking lot, give him or her a call to see if the agent is inside working (safety in numbers).
- Park in a well-lit front lot and enter and exit the building from the front door only. Never enter a door that cannot be seen by people driving by.
- As you approach the office door, pull it to ensure it is locked before you use your office key. If it is not locked, *do not enter* and call police.
- Once safely inside, ensure the door locks behind you and disarm the building alarm. Depending on the alarm settings, you may be able reset the alarm while inside the building.
- Check other doors and see if other agents are working, too.
- Let someone know you are working late at the office and have this person periodically give you a call on your cell phone to check up.
- If applicable, follow company policy regarding office occupancy after hours.

- If clients meet you at the office to conduct business, do not inform them you are alone in the office.
- When leaving the office, notify anyone else working in the office and also call your safety contact to let him or her know you are leaving. Look out windows and doors for anyone hanging around in the parking lot before you open the door.
- If you feel unsafe for any reason, call the police to escort you from the property.
- Have your self-defense plan in mind just in case you need it.

Location of Office

As a real-estate professional, have you ever considered where your office is located? Is your office in or near a designated high-crime area of your city? Is it in a commercial district with other commercial businesses, bars, or restaurants? Or, on a busy street or bypass or near a busy interstate exchange? Or is your main or satellite office located in a remote area with few people, buildings, or houses nearby? Take a moment to evaluate where you work each day and the area surrounding your office as you develop your personal safety plan.

Designated High-Crime Area

Be aware that criminals do travel by vehicle and on foot looking for easy targets and will lay in wait for the right opportunity. Common crimes are usually purse snatching, robbery, car theft, and carjacking; violent crimes usually associated with robberies. If your office is located in such an area, your parking lot is a prime location for such crimes.

Commercial District

Districts comprised of office suites with standard office days and hours can be lonely, deserted areas after hours and on weekends when the real-estate professional may be working. Be wary when entering and exiting your office during these times.

Are bars and restaurants located near your office? If so, it may not be uncommon for strange vehicles to be parked in your parking lot after hours, and there may be occasional encounters with an intoxicated person when you attempt to enter or leave your office after hours.

Busy Street

Criminals will chose locations that can be accessed easily, with a clear getaway route to a busy street. Their primary goal is to complete the crime and escape undetected into the crowd.

Remote Office Locations

The most dangerous location is an office or satellite office located in a remote area and occupied by one person. In one of the case studies, two real-estate professionals were killed in a satellite office located in a sparsely populated development. The offender knew the office was manned by one person and the office door was always open to potential clients. Criminals always look for a one-on-one confrontation when selecting a victim to ensure success and escape undetected.

Office Design Considerations

Office Landscape

Be aware of the landscape surrounding your office—whether it includes bushes, flower beds, large trash bins, or open areas. Note the topography of those open areas: they provide potential hiding places for the criminal to lie in wait for unsuspecting victims.

Another consideration, which is seldom considered, is how a criminal may approach an area on foot. Not all criminals use vehicles to move in and out of crime areas. Check your office area for large drainage ditches, railroad tracks, and rights-of-way, which can be used by criminals to move in and around an area undetected.

Office Parking-Lot Safety Tips

Parking lots are prime locations for criminals to accost victims as they exit or enter buildings or vehicles. Burdened with paperwork, briefcases, and large purses and bags, real-estate professionals become easy targets as they enter or exit their offices. Parking the car and entering the building become habitual movements, with little thought given to safety. Here are some things to remember about parking-lot safety:

- Attempt to park at or near the front entrance to the building if possible, especially after hours.
- After hours, circle the entire building before parking, and pay close attention to strangers or strange vehicles around the building.
- Outside lighting is an important safety consideration after hours and in the early morning. *Notify your building owners/ broker immediately if outside lights are inoperable.*
- Pay close attention to occupied vehicles parked in the parking lot.
- People not conducting business should not be allowed to loiter on the office parking lot at any time. However, it is safer not to park than to confront strangers in the parking lot.

- Make several trips to your vehicle to unload bulky items rather than be loaded down and unable to resist an attack or flee from the area.

Office Floor Plan

It is important to know your entire office floor plan in case you must hide, barricade yourself, or evacuate.

We have all seen media accounts of disgruntled ex-employees, spouses, ex-spouses, or customers who have attacked an office and everyone inside to make a point. Because of his or her state of mind, the attacker usually has no fear of being injured or killed as a result of the attack. And usually, the attacker has no fear of harming or murdering anyone in the building who may confront him or her.

Office Safety Tips

- Management should consider having a written safety plan and conduct regular trainings on how to deal with office threats.
- The front office receptionist should be equipped with a panic button, alarm, or signal of some type to alert people in the building of a possible threat. Personnel should be trained on how to respond to the emergency signal.
- Locate each exit door in the office and know how to open it. Most doors are equipped with push-type handles or crash bars; however, some doors must be opened with a key (especially after hours).
- Lock up your valuables when away from your work area.
- Be familiar with your office door and windows in case you must barricade yourself during an attack. Does the door

lock, and does the lock actually work? Are the windows fixed or locked, or do they open enough to provide an escape route?

- Be aware of unusually loud talking, arguing, or loud noises not usually heard in your office. You will know when something out of the norm is taking place. Retreat to a safe place and call the police.
- Do not take threatening calls lightly. If someone threatens to come to your office to cause harm, report the call to the police immediately.
- Fire and smoke are also threats while inside your office building. The smoke produced by fire is the real danger to people trying to exit the building. Stay close to the floor (under the smoke) and use your knowledge of the building to make your escape.

Summary

Your office building should be a safe haven for you to conduct your daily business—and usually it is exactly that. However, things can go deadly wrong at the office too. Although management may have emergency plans and procedures, if there is no periodic safety training or the plans are not followed or rehearsed, they do little good. I would strongly recommend that you take the responsibility to devise a commonsense personal office safety plan.

CHAPTER 10

Self-Defense and the Justice System

I am always asked by real-estate professionals during my safety seminars about self-defense and what weapons I would recommend they carry. My answer is the same each time I am asked, "It depends, and I am not an attorney." Much thought and consideration must be used when employing self-defense techniques or carrying a self-defense weapon. You take on a huge responsibility when you decide to carry a weapon, especially a firearm.

Many states allow citizens to legally carry concealed firearms with a valid permit. In fact, you may have a client who has a concealed carry permit and may be armed when he or she shows up for a showing. But just because someone is armed does not mean he or she intends to harm you. It is very important for you to know your state law regarding carrying concealed weapons. Consulting with an attorney when you are considering a concealed carry permit is always a good idea.

If you use self-defense techniques or a weapon, how will the criminal, federal, or civil courts view your actions? You, as a private citizen, must meet the same standard as any police officer when using force against another person. According to our criminal laws, any battery on another person is illegal in America. If you batter another person, you can expect to be arrested and prosecuted, and that person or his family could bring a civil suit against you for damages resulting from the harm or loss you inflicted—even if you were, initially, the victim.

On the other hand, criminal law does provide you with the right to defend yourself if you are in fear of your life or great bodily harm, or are protecting someone else who is in danger. However, depending on the incident, a trial may be required, and a jury may be impaneled to determine if the facts of the case proved a reasonable person would have done the same thing you did to protect yourself or someone else. This doctrine is known as the "reasonable man theory." Regardless of the finding of a criminal jury, a civil claim for damages could also result in a separate trial proceeding.

Use of Weapons

Weapons come in many shapes and sizes. A weapon is simply anything that can be used to cause bodily harm. An old police officer told me he lived by one very important rule, "Never take a knife to a gun fight." Many people assume weapons to mean only guns and knives, but actually, almost anything can be used as a weapon.

The choice of weapon used during a crime determines the severity and punishment of the crime. Weapons are often classified as lethal and nonlethal. Lethal weapons are those designed to kill or inflict serious injury, such as guns and knives. Nonlethal weapons are weapons not expected to inflict fatal injuries, such as mace, stun guns, hands, and so on. If a person uses a gun or knife, it would be very difficult to claim that his or her intent was not to kill or inflict great bodily harm.

Know Your Personality: Fight or Flight

We all have unique personalities that define who we are as a person. Most people are not hardwired to hurt anyone or anything intentionally. Some people cannot stand the sight of blood or dislike any kind of altercation and will simply give up or try to avoid tense situations. But we are all hardwired to survive.

The important questions are: What are you willing to do if you are attacked and are forced to fight for your life or die? You must realize if you do fight back, it is almost certain you will be injured. Will you be able to stay in the fight with injuries or will you surrender? What single thing do you value most to fight to the death to survive? You are the only person who can answer these questions, and it is important that you develop the proper survival mind-set.

While considering these questions, keep it simple and think about it often. I have the same philosophy today as a real-estate agent as I did during my law-enforcement career. My main goal is to come home to my family every day, and I will do anything necessary to accomplish that goal. I realize I have many years of police training focused on street survival to aid me if faced with a life-and-death situation. However, you, too, can take self-defense classes to help you gain confidence in your survival abilities and discover what physical and mental limits you possess.

There are also those times when your best option will be flight instead of fighting your attacker. There is no shame in running from your attacker if given the opportunity. Any survival technique is a win when you survive. Putting space and other people between you and the attacker can be the best plan and works better in an outside location. But keep one thing in mind: if you fail to escape, you will have used up valuable energy, which will put you at a disadvantage if you are forced to revert to a self-defense mode.

The point is to have an overpowering reason to survive and be prepared to do whatever you must do to survive. I can assure you any criminal you may encounter already has his survival mode on high alert; his intent is to do his deed and flee undetected, just like the shark feeding in the sea.

The Law and Use of Weapons

Is my chosen weapon absolutely necessary to save a life in my situation? This is the key question to ask yourself when considering the use of a weapon against another human being, particularly a lethal weapon. You will be required to answer this same question in front of a criminal or civil jury.

Does the attacker have to be armed to justify lethal force? Under certain circumstances, the attacker does *not* need to be armed. However, the legal test must be considered, documented, and proven. For the act to be justified, the circumstances must be articulated in such a fashion that the ordinary, reasonable man would have come to the same conclusion as you did if placed in the same situation.

For example, if you are being choked to death by an unarmed attacker, lethal force could be justified to stop the attack. Other factors to be considered are the size of the attacker versus the size of the victim, the actions of the attacker, the distance between the victim and the attacker, threatening statements made by the attacker, statements made by the victim, and any injuries inflicted upon the victim.

You cannot undo your actions after the fact. During my years as a police officer, I faced many incidents where I would have been legally justified to use lethal force against an offender, but thanks to my training, the nonlethal force I used was enough to subdue the perpetrators on all but one occasion. Unfortunately, most people do not have the law-enforcement training to deal with attackers and may unnecessarily resort to lethal force to stop an attack.

Lethal force should be the *last resort* to save your life or the life of another person; if there is any other option, you should avoid lethal force. Otherwise, be prepared to justify your actions in a court of law. Although you may use lethal force, you may only seriously injure the offender, and he or she may retreat. If the offender does retreat, the situation is over, and further use of force on your part will not be justified unless the attacker's actions place you in fear of your life again by reengaging in the attack. Remember, when you are no longer in danger, any use of continued force cannot be justified.

What is legally considered a weapon? Attorneys could argue this question for days! Don't be confused when thinking about weapons; simply stated, a weapon is anything used to cause bodily harm or death. A writing pen can be used as a weapon. In fact, many real-estate professionals have used their pens as weapons to fend off attackers. We all carry items that can be effectively used as weapons. I am certified with a Kubaton and carry one attached to my key ring every single day. Car keys are handy weapons if you know how to use them. Think about what you carry and include it in your personal safety plan.

If you decide to carry a weapon, do not do so until you have been trained and certified by a professional instructor. Do not depend on a nonprofessional to teach you about the use, handling, and firing of a gun. There are professional instructors in every city who, for a fee, train and certify people to use all types of weapons. And some trainers offer self-defense training, too. Don't overlook self-defense training skills because, in certain situations, you may need to know both types of techniques. One thing to keep in mind about training: if you ever stand in front of a jury, it is better to have updated training than not. One last thing about training: if you do not practice the skills learned, you will be less likely to depend on them when needed.

At this point, I must once again issue my disclaimer: I am not an attorney, and I do not give legal advice! I would strongly recommend you retain an attorney if you do not have one already. If you are considering or are already carrying a concealed weapon, talk with your attorney about the laws regulating carrying and using weapons for self-defense in your state. The laws for each state are quite different. Concealed firearm carry/concealment laws have strict requirements from state to state, and it is your responsibility to know the laws of your state. Ignorance of the law is no defense.

Ask your attorney about your rights if you are involved in a situation. Make sure you use an attorney who will respond to your request for help after normal working hours or on holidays if you need emergency legal services. Make no statement without your attorney at your side.

Lethal Weapons

As discussed, any weapon intentionally used to inflict great bodily harm or death is considered a lethal weapon. The most common lethal weapons real-estate professionals come in contact with are guns and knives. Our case studies indicated guns and knives are most often used against real-estate professionals. However, hands can also be used as lethal weapons by those who have extensive knowledge of hand-to-hand tactics.

As for firearms, there are all types and calibers of guns on the market. It may become necessary to give the police a description of a weapon used by an attacker. To provide an accurate description, you should know the differences between an automatic weapon and a revolver. A revolver has a wheel mechanism that holds the bullets to be fired. You can actually see the bullets if the weapon is pointed at you. An automatic weapon is sleek, and no bullets are visible.

Handguns can be different colors. Some are blue steel, and some are chrome-plated steel. It is very important for the police to know the type and finish of a weapon used in a crime just in case they unknowingly stop the suspect after the attack, and the attacker is in possession of the weapon you described. Take a field trip to your local sporting goods store and look at the handguns to learn the differences between each type of weapon. Store clerks will be happy to explain and show you the types of firearms available.

Knife attacks are fast and usually deadly. The knife is a popular weapon for several reasons. They are much easier to obtain, far less expensive than a firearm, require no type of governmental registration, can be carried legally if it meets state law requirements, are easy to conceal, and are deadly if used by a person who has the knowledge and ability to use it.

The knife is also the weapon of choice by those offenders who have been forbidden to carry firearms because of prior criminal convictions. According to Dennis Tueller, an expert in the field, it takes an attacker wielding a knife approximately 1.5 seconds to attack a victim from an unobstructed distance of twenty-one feet. Conversely, using a firearm, it takes more than 1.5 seconds to draw, fire, and hit a target at seven yards.

Nonlethal Weapons

As we discussed earlier in the chapter, nonlethal weapons are weapons not expected to cause great bodily harm. These weapons are popular as distraction devices to back an attacker down into retreat mode. The most common nonlethal weapons are pepper spray, mace, Kubotans, and stun guns, all of which are readily available to the public and easily concealed.

The same training recommendations apply to these weapons. Seek out a professional trainer to help you understand exactly how to use these weapons and practice, practice, practice. I should warn you to be careful with pepper spray and mace products. Unfortunately, if used during an attack, both you and the attacker will likely receive a good dose of the spray, and it may render you helpless as well. And remember, if and when the offender retreats, the further use of weapons cannot be justified unless the aggressor resumes the attack.

The ultimate self-defense weapon is the firearm, and the user must be prepared to fire the weapon until the *aggression stops*. I hope you never have to use a firearm in self-defense. If you do, please do not be under the false impression that if you just fire once, the bad guy will instantly fall over and that will be the end of the attack—like in an old cowboy movie. That never happens; it may take many rounds to finally stop an attacker. This is why you hear reports of law enforcement shooting someone multiple times to finally stop the aggression.

There is no guarantee that any other self-defense weapon will be as effective and, in fact, may only serve to anger the attacker to the point of causing the victim certain injury or death. However, in a desperate situation, it is better to at least have some sort of weapon than not.

Office Regulations

If you are considering carrying a weapon, consult with your manager or broker to determine if the office has a policy prohibiting the possession of a weapon inside or outside the office. Abide by your office policy to the letter because you are responsible and liable for any mishaps involving a weapon.

Summary

Self-defense is a very important issue to consider for anyone involved in real estate. Many decisions must be made before an attack. Do I carry a weapon? Do I simply run in the event of an attack? Do I use hand-to-hand techniques to defend myself? Do I have the toughness to engage in a fight to save my life? Do I even have a self-defense plan?

Consult with an attorney to fully understand the laws of your state regarding carrying self-defense weapons, firearms, and legal justified self-defense options. If you decide to carry a weapon after your legal consultation, immediately enroll in some form of certified training with a professional and document and practice the self-defense skills you have learned. In the worst-case scenario, make sure your attorney will be available if you need emergency legal advice.

Always remember that during an attack, when the aggression stops and/or you have disabled the attacker, reasonable force means *you must stop further use of force.* Further use of force on your part cannot be justified, and your actions become illegal if the attacker is disabled and no longer a threat. Discuss use of force with your attorney.

CHAPTER 11

The Aftermath of an Attack

Being the victim of a criminal attack is a traumatic experience for anyone. Most people will never be a victim or be required to interact closely with law enforcement. And because most people can reasonably expect never to be victims, they have no idea how to interact with law enforcement when an attack does happen.

Law-enforcement officers must rely on the victim to provide enough detailed information about the crime so that they can gather sufficient evidence to eventually make an arrest. If law enforcement has any chance of making an arrest and building a solid criminal case, the victim must provide immediate accurate and detailed information.

The criminal justice system reacts differently when you become a victim and do not defend yourself with a weapon versus when you defend yourself and kill or injure an attacker. And what happens if you are critically injured or abducted and can't tell your story? What must you include in your safety plan to account for these various situations?

You Are the Victim

Immediately Report the Incident to the Police

You will most likely be the person who notifies the police by cell phone. The attacker will usually flee the scene in fear of being arrested. Remain at the scene, if it is a safe area, and try to calm yourself down before calling 911.

The 911 operator will ask "What is your emergency?" and ask for your exact location. It will be imperative for you to speak clearly and for you to know the exact address. The operator will ask you many other questions, but do not become impatient: the operator is dispatching help and any necessary medical emergency services as you are talking. Remember that what you say to authorities is being recorded and could later be used against you if you misspeak.

The police response may not be immediate. Response times vary with every law-enforcement agency across the country. Depending on logistics, it could take ten to fifteen minutes or longer for an officer to arrive on the scene.

While waiting for first responders, do not touch or move anything inside the crime scene because everything is evidence. It is best to wait outside the crime scene if possible to preserve important evidence.

If you are armed or have a concealed weapon, advise the responding officer immediately and have your carry permit ready.

When emergency response personnel arrive, the crime scene can become confusing. During the confusion, the responding officer will want a quick statement from you that the officer can then broadcast to other officers to aid them in the apprehension of the offender. The first hour after the attack is a critical time period for law enforcement to apprehend the attacker on the street as he or she flees the area.

The police will need to gather as much information as possible from you about the suspect(s). They will ask who, what, when, where, and how questions to aid them in their investigation. Try to remain as calm as possible and give complete and accurate information. Do not talk to anyone other than the responding officer on the scene.

Depending on the situation, the media may respond to the scene or contact you to obtain information. You are not required to give a media statement, and I would strongly recommend you not speak with the media or allow a spokesperson, other than your legal representative, to speak on your behalf under any circumstance.

Critical First-Responder Information

Think of beneficial information to aid the police in their efforts to apprehend the suspect(s). Many times a victim may remember or discover documented information days or weeks after the criminal event. Immediately notify the police of any material facts of the crime. As real-estate professionals, we collect documents, notes, and client information, which may be vitally important to investigating officers.

- **Accurate personal notes you have made about your client.** You may have copied the client's driver's license or received letters from his or her lending institution; those documents are in your file and may help identify the attacker.
- **A description of what happened.** You must verbalize exactly what happened and what the suspect said during the commission of the criminal act. Days later you may remember a critical fact that will benefit the investigation.
- **A detailed description of the attacker.** In your description, include his or her approximate weight and height, hair and eye color, and any distinguishing scars, marks, or tattoos. Make a mental picture of anyone you come in contact with.

You may be required to identify your attacker from a live police lineup or a photo array at some point.

- **A description of the attacker's clothing.** Give a complete description of the attacker's clothing, including footwear, at the time of the attack.
- **A detailed description of the weapon.** If you have familiarized yourself with firearms as I suggested, you should be able to give a good description, such as "a large caliber automatic pistol with a wooden handle and a chrome finish."
- **Information about the attacker's vehicle.** If the attacker drove his vehicle to the scene, you should make notes that include the license plate number and type, model, approximate year, and color of the vehicle. Also make note of any distinguishing features of the vehicle such as dents, broken windows, and so on.
- **Information about your car, if stolen.** If you drove the attacker to the scene and your car was stolen by the attacker, know your license plate number; the make, model, and year of your vehicle; and your vehicle registration number. A photo of your vehicle is also useful.
- **Descriptions or photos of personal property and credit-card numbers.** Attackers often steal credit cards, debit cards, purses, cash, and jewelry. It is important that you have access to your credit-card numbers and have descriptions or photos of personal items taken.
- **A printed list of expenditures on your credit or bank cards.** Law enforcement has the technology to track credit-card expenditures if the criminal uses them to travel out of the area.
- **Information about interactions with attacker.** Advise police if any of your colleagues or other witnesses interacted with the attacker. Anyone who had contact with the suspect may be able to provide valuable information and descriptions.

- **Identification of your weapon.** If you have a weapon, let the responding officer know immediately for his or her and your own safety. If it is a concealed firearm, be sure to produce your concealed carry permit if required by your state. Once again, know your concealed carry rights established by your state.

Self-Defense: Lethal Force by the Agent

It is necessary to consider a worst-case scenario for you, the real-estate professional, which is the attacker(s) or suspect(s) being killed or seriously injured by you while defending yourself. If you reach this point, you have made the decision to carry a self-defense weapon and are now responsible for your actions. Expect to be arrested; in fact, some states require an arrest to be made. But do not panic or make any wild statements you will later regret.

As we discussed earlier, you are held to the same standards as a law-enforcement officer when he or she uses force to protect his or her life or someone else's life. You must be absolutely sure your actions justified the force you used to protect yourself or another person. You may face criminal and possible personal civil action against you, and you may need to prove that you acted as any other reasonable person would have acted if placed in the same situation.

It is important for you to understand how police respond to and investigate potential homicide cases in order for you to make the right personal decisions.

Law-Enforcement Investigative Response

Are You a Victim or a Suspect?

If you are involved in a situation resulting in a homicide and you caused the death or injury, you could not only be the victim of the crime but also a suspect in the homicide if the offender dies as a result.

How can you be both victim and suspect? The statement sounds confusing, to say the least. You will have to prove that lethal force was justified. Simply put, by compiling and presenting the relevant facts of the incident, the evidence must prove that you were the unfortunate victim and acted reasonably while defending yourself.

Police

Every law-enforcement officer is trained to treat each case as if it is the worst-case scenario. They must remain 100 percent neutral and collect the facts. The investigative facts will later prove exactly what happened and investigative evidence will prevail.

Remember that *nothing is off the record*: anything you say can and will be used for or against you. Police must document exactly what you and any other witness may say regarding the incident. It would be wise for you to inform officers that you will be happy to give a statement after you speak with your attorney.

Prosecution

Law-enforcement officers investigate all such cases as homicides and later submit all documented investigative reports to their respective prosecuting agency.

If during the investigation, law-enforcement investigators determine there is probable cause to believe the force used did not justify the death or injury, you will be arrested and held pending a release bond set by a judge.

Depending on the circumstances, the law-enforcement agency may elect to complete the investigation and submit the case to the prosecuting agency to determine if enough probable cause exists for an arrest or an arrest warrant.

Grand Jury

The prosecuting agency may elect to submit the case facts to a grand jury made up of citizens to decide if an arrest is justified and if the case is to be prosecuted.

Only the prosecuting agency or a grand jury, after a complete review of the evidence, may decide if you should be held for trial on the charges or amend the charges. Each jurisdiction throughout the United States has different procedures for handling criminal cases, and you should consult with your attorney.

Civil Actions

Apart from criminal actions, civil actions could also be lodged against someone who injures or kills another person. These actions are taken up in a civil court, and monetary sanctions can be imposed to those involved in the action.

Typical complaints could be loss of income, loss of career, loss of support, and/or loss of mental or physical career abilities. The criminal or his family on his behalf could actually bring an action against the victim.

Serious Long-Term Situation

However, regardless of the jurisdiction, the point is that any time a person is injured or killed; it becomes a serious, long-term legal situation involving attorneys and courts of law and will be extremely expensive. The battle could last for years.

Note: It is extremely important to involve your attorney immediately if you are involved in such a situation. Refrain from making any detailed statements to anyone, especially the media, without legal counsel. Anything you say may and will be used against you in a court of law. Your attorney can advise you each step of the way to ensure your rights are safeguarded.

Injury or Abduction of the Real-Estate Professional

What happens when you are severely injured or abducted? The worst-case scenario would be if you were attacked and left to die without anyone knowing your whereabouts. Once again, I cannot stress enough how important it is to let someone know where you are going and with whom and when you will return, at the very minimum. And fight to death before you allow anyone to abduct you.

Robbery is usually the motive when a real-estate professional is attacked, as the case examples demonstrated. However, sexual attacks are many times a secondary motive along with robbery. The "Critical First-Responder Checklist" will do little good if you are totally incapacitated, unresponsive, or abducted. Law enforcement must have immediate information from someone to begin the investigation in an effort to capture the suspect(s) and retrieve the victim; time is the difference between death and survival.

Incapacitated or Abducted Victim Checklist

- The first order of business will be to obtain emergency medical treatment for the victim (if still on the scene). If the victim is unconscious, little information will be available for law enforcement to begin the investigation until the victim can speak or communicate.
- In the case of a sexual attack, it will be necessary for medical personnel to collect evidence from the victim. Unfortunately, this procedure is needed to prove there was a sexual attack and to obtain DNA evidence to possibly identify the suspect. Do not destroy evidence by changing clothes, taking a bath or shower, or attempting to wash up.
- It is vitally important to plan ahead and compile important information that will aid law enforcement. Ensure a

responsible person has a contact list of who to call in case of emergency. The designee should be informed immediately upon notification of an emergency.

- Ensure the emergency contact has a list of your current medical doctors and attorneys and your requested hospital, along with telephone numbers.
- Compile a list, copies, or photos of your valuable personal belongings, including credit and bank cards, driver's license, personal checks, jewelry, and cell phone.
- Include several large personal photographs in case you are abducted. Make sure the emergency contact has the photos ready for release.
- Photograph all four sides of the vehicle normally used while conducting real-estate business.
- Provide the emergency contact a copy of your vehicle registration, including owner information, vehicle identification number (VIN), and license plate number. If your vehicle is taken during the attack, this information will be needed immediately by law enforcement.
- Advise the emergency contact if the vehicle is equipped with the OnStar vehicle locator system and how to enable the system to locate the vehicle.
- A computer-scanned file with all the above personal information would be useful if law enforcement needs immediate access to the information in case of emergency.
- Law enforcement has the technology to place a local and national be-on-the-lookout for the victim's vehicle and purchases or withdrawals using personal accounts and credit cards.
- Keep updated client, contact, and customer files. Law enforcement will search for clues to identify the attacker(s) if the victim is not responsive or has been abducted.

- If an iPhone is carried, be sure that the "find my phone" feature of the device is activated. This may lead emergency responders to you or the suspect.

Summary

Most people live their entire lives without becoming involved in a serious, life-threatening situation involving law enforcement. But it is wise to be aware of what to expect from law enforcement when and if things go terribly wrong. The response and investigative checklists outline what to expect during the criminal investigation and what information may be needed from you, as a victim.

Expect law enforcement to respond with a critical eye and a neutral opinion of the situation. You can expect the responding officers to only want your statement and offer no positive or negative feedback as to your actions. This may seem to be a suspicious, cold, and disrespectful attitude toward your situation, but I assure you, it is not. After caring for the injured and securing the scene, law enforcement will be responsible for putting facts together quickly to notify other officers and agencies in an effort to apprehend the suspect.

It is the victim's responsibility—or that of his or her emergency representative, if the victim is incapacitated or abducted—to supply as many facts as possible to law enforcement to properly investigate the incident. To begin compiling needed personal information during a confusing emergency event is almost impossible and wastes precious investigative time. In the case of abduction, the victim has only hours to survive in most cases and time will determine life or death.

Use the checklists to document and update your important information as the foundation of your personal safety plan before an emergency situation arises. And make sure your emergency representatives have or can retrieve your personal information immediately if needed. I can only hope this information will never be needed, and you only waste some time compiling it.

Remember, time is of the essence and as time passes, the likelihood of capturing the suspect or rescuing an abducted victim is severely diminished.

Lastly, if you have decided to carry a self-defense weapon, have attended training, and have become proficient in the use of the weapon, you must understand the legal constraints concerning use of force against another person. Carrying a weapon places strict legal responsibilities on the person who carries, and lasting psychological, financial, and legal burdens may occur if the weapon is used in a self-defense situation.

If a death results because of your use of force, it is important to understand the steps of the homicide investigation and resulting legal proceedings as the case proceeds through the criminal and civil courts—sometimes for years. Rely on your attorney to guide you through the process by safeguarding your constitutional rights. However, do not let fear of the end result prevent you from *surviving in real estate.*

NOTES

NOTES

NOTES

NOTES

NOTES

NOTES

NOTES

NOTES

NOTES

NOTES